The Positive Coaching Movement

James Devlin

ACKNOWLEDGMENTS

Firstly, thank you to my beautiful family, Sonia, Isla, Wyatt, and Ezra. I love you all so much and am inspired to be better because of you all.
Thank you to my parents for always encouraging me to follow my dreams and a big thank you to mum for helping with early drafts and edits.
Thank you to all the coaches I have worked with over the years. There are far too many to list but I have learned from each and every one of you.
Thank you to all of the gymnasts I have coached, in particular Cleo, Adele, Elise and Amber who provided me with valuable feedback on my own coaching so I could improve.
Thank you to the team I work with including all Jets Managers plus Aley and Tim who I work with everyday and help shape my thoughts and values.
As a Christian I thank God, my faith is my key motivator to do good things for others.

A massive thank you again to my amazing wife Sonia, not only did you support me in writing this book, you also dealt with the kids while I was out and on top of it all have edited every single word in your spare time. You are truly an amazing woman of many talents and I will always treasure you.

If you like this book the credit goes to Sonia.

i

1 INTRODUCTION

Hi and welcome to my book. Firstly, let me introduce myself, my name is James Devlin and I am currently General Manager for Jets Gymnastics. I have taught athletes of all ages throughout my career and believe I have found a particularly successful style of coaching I want to share with you. These methods are not only effective in enhancing individual performance, but for creating enjoyment and meaningful lives beyond the sport of the gymnasts. I am sharing some of the strategies that I use, not so coaches can be like me or produce athletes like mine, but so they can feel the fulfillment I feel with my career. I have been in gymnastics since I was five years old and have been coaching and working in the sport for eighteen years. It's through my career as a coach that I have come to believe that gymnastics, and sport in general, could benefit from the techniques and engaging coaching style that I have been so lucky to learn.

I feel a coach is someone who has a huge responsibility. Not only do they need to teach their sport, but they are also able to inspire success, teach life lessons and empower athletes to be the absolute best version of themselves. The truth is coaches have the power to influence for good or bad. They can contribute to producing the most amazing, well-adjusted person, or can also contribute to lasting mental health issues. These outcomes can come from both conscious and unconscious decisions made by a coach. It is for this reason, that I think as coaches we absolutely must be intentional about everything that we do. This is our most important responsibility.

As an NHL fan myself, nothing highlights to me the importance of a coach more than the Pittsburg Penguin's season in 2009. They started off extremely well, but slowly declined in performance, getting worse and worse each game until, after a devastating 6-2 loss to the Maple Leafs, their head coach, Michel Therrien, was relieved from his position. Therrien was replaced by Dan Bylsma in the middle of the NHL season who was only thirty-eight years old, the youngest coach at that time in the NHL. Under Bylsma's guidance, the Penguins went on to win eighteen of the next twenty-five games and won the Stanley Cup in the same year. This story illustrates the significant impact one person can make on an athlete's success in a relatively short amount time. Every sport, at the top level, has specialized development paths and different training techniques for the journey to success.

My sport, gymnastics, is an individual sport that presents athlete's top skills to a panel of judges who score their performances. Judges deduct points from athletes based on how well their skills are executed. Gymnastics is a sport that has one of the most dramatic increase in abilities from entry level to the top. When athletes start out in gymnastics, it's likely that performing a simple cartwheel is difficult. Compare this to a double twisting double back somersault, which you may see preformed at Olympic level, and you can see the significant journey of skill that athlete has accomplished. If you are not already a gymnastics coach, you can probably imagine the number of hours and work involved in getting to that very complex level. This means a significant number of hours spent between athlete and coach to reach these shared goals. That is why in my opinion it's the perfect sport to highlight the individual struggles and the psychological effects that a coach has on their athletes.

I am not a gymnastics coaching expert. My insights come from my experiences in coaching preschoolers through to gymnasts in a high level. I have not coached at an international level. I do strongly believe however that coaching at all levels has some basic principles that can be applied for success. This book presents insights I have learned through experience, observation, talking to gymnasts, a survey of my own design completed by over 100 competitive level gymnasts and other research surrounding the influence of a coach. I believe firstly, and whole heartedly, in being positive to all athletes I coach. I hope that this book can speak to other coaches in a positive way, offering some practical tools to enable your athletes to become the best possible versions of themselves as both an athlete, but more importantly, as a person.

One of the key motivators for me to write this book comes from discussions I've had with ex gymnasts, some who are friends and some who I have encountered through circumstance. One thing that was clear in these interactions, is that instead of sharing positive experiences they predominantly shared negative experiences that they had with a coach or coaches. In fact, several of them were currently suffering with mental health problems that they in part attributed to the role of their coach. This shocked me and was the motivation behind my survey, I wanted to know if this was just a few experiences or if it was a wider spread issue. The results will be shared in more depth throughout the book, but I was startled to learn that only eight percent of gymnasts who completed the survey would recommend friends or family to do gymnastics to the same level as they had. That is not a result that comes from athletes who have been bettered by their experience with their coaches and the sport, but from those who look back and think their sport did them more harm than good.

So many coaches are passionate about their sport and well intentioned, but evidently there are coaching techniques that can ultimately cause lifelong harm to an individual. I believe small changes can be made to make a big difference and increase the joy of participation in sport and people's lives.

2 THE ROLE OF A COACH

To start off this chapter I wanted to share my own personal experience being a gymnast. My involvement in gymnastics began as the result of being part of a 'gymnastics' family. My sister was aiming to be an Olympic gymnast and was sure she was going to make it; my mum was a coach and started her own business teaching gymnastics in schools and my dad did whatever he could to support the family gymnastics dream. I started out doing gymnastics at the same club that my sister trained at, and mother worked, and I certainly didn't love it to start with. I was a stop start gymnast, taking some time off and then returning to give it another go, but the boys program at this club was all recreational and I was ready for a challenge. Luckily, just before I quit again, I was moved to a nearby gym with a bigger, more challenging, boys' program.

I enjoyed my time at the new club and got along

well with the coach. I was still however a very unmotivated gymnast for the level I was in and would often miss sessions if I had a better offer, especially every Friday night when I could go to the school disco. A key difference that this program offered was an award that was given to one deserving gymnast at the end of the week, called 'gymnast of the week'. I wanted to stay in the group and worked hard for positive feedback and praise from my coach when I was in class, hoping it would lead to me getting the award.

Fast forward a couple of years, my mum's business started managing a gymnastics club, so I moved again and joined this club's squad program. Once again, I wasn't that committed, but this time there was no 'gymnast of the week' to strive for and there was a lot of pressure to perform well. It wasn't long until I was asking to quit. Thankfully my parents had a better plan and moved me to a recreational based competitive program. It was in this group where I found my passion and drive for gymnastics, not through a new love for the sport, but because I found my 'tribe' amongst the other kids in my group. I very quickly became best friends with everyone and remain great friends with some of them to this day. In fact, my best friend was in this group and is such a good friend that he gave me permission to marry his sister.

When I look back on my own gymnastics career, I don't think about the speeches my coaches gave, the corrections they made or the lessons they tried to teach me. I think about two things, my successes at competitions, in particular the team awards, and far more importantly I think about the people, the friends

I made and the fun we had together. We were having so much fun, we all started coming to gym straight from school, which was two hours early, and would just hang out together before training. We also had a coach that fostered this group dynamic by allowing us to be ourselves and coached us in a way that met us exactly where we were in life. Which unfortunately for him, that stage was being a hormone surging teenage boy who found enjoyment in playing pranks. We perhaps went too far those times we removed his car's hub caps or ambushed him, tying him up and leaving him unable to free himself. Looking back, the amazing thing is that Paul was never angry and always laughed with us, simply making sure it didn't get too out of hand. This relationship we built with each other and with our good-natured coach was a significant factor in me forming my coaching philosophy.

I'm not saying that a coach should be the victim of an athlete's pranks, that is definitely not what people sign up for. What I am saying is that no matter how good a coach you are, your gymnasts won't remember the specific things you've said or the lessons you teach, they will remember the experience they had. Most importantly, they will remember whether that experience was negative or positive. If you truly want to influence an athlete's life, then as a coach the key is to focus on the experiences you create for them.

A good coach has the power to shape an athlete's future. Great experiences will be looked back on fondly as a great time in their lives, but a bad experience can potentially lead to significant problems in the athlete's life. As previously mentioned, while researching for this book I spoke to many gymnasts that have mental health related issues, which they attribute to the high pressure and negative experiences that they had as gymnasts. What is most heart breaking is I believe all coaches actually want the complete opposite for their athletes. In fact, they all coach because they believe they are doing good in the athlete's lives and would likely be devastated knowing of such significant negative impacts.

Stephanie Moorhouse was an athlete who competed for Australia in the 2004 Olympics and was on the gold medal team for the 2002 Commonwealth Games. She is currently the Performance Health & AMS Manager at Gymnastics Australia. While talking to Steph she gave some great insight from an elite athlete's view, "I think the coach is seen as an important mentor and influential role model in an athlete's life, and sometimes, I think the coach can forget how significant they are to an athlete. The constant feedback and time spent with the coach, can shape how the athlete develops and flourishes, or struggles throughout their life." The survey I conducted with over 100 high level gymnasts gave us further insight into these impacts of a coach. In this survey, only 8% of the gymnasts would recommend for someone else to do gymnastics at the same level they had. That means that 92% of these gymnasts wouldn't want people to experience what they had. These statistics tell us that those gymnasts experiences were not positive, and most likely have not helped them to live a better life.

I believe these results show us that coaches have a

real impact in kid's lives, and we have the opportunity to change that to be a positive one. This book gives coaches practical steps in making changes to positively shape the future of the athletes they coach. These steps are particularly impacting in gymnastics, but I feel can be applied to all sports. Before we get into those steps let's talk about the role of the coach. There are three things that I believe defines our job as a coach.

Number 1: Improve the life of athletes.

I have a good friend, Mary-Anne Monckton, who was an elite level athlete representing Australia at multiple world championships and Commonwealth Games. She is now a coach of squad athletes herself, and her mantra is 'people first, gymnastics second'. I have always been inspired by this, I think it's a simple thing you can repeat to yourself over and over, so you remember that there is more to life, for these athletes, than just the sport they are doing. A simple way to think about this is, if the sport is their entire life and their happiness depends on it, what happens if they get injured and can't do it anymore? Or their parents can no longer afford it? Without the personal skills to deal with the disappointment, losing the ability to do their sport can have a far more negative impact than it needs to.

There are a couple of practical things as coaches we should be doing to ensure our athletes know they are people first and are more important than the sport they are doing. In my experience I have seen some coaches issue punishment when life gets in the way of the sport. For example, if a gymnast is late, they may be forced to do extra strength or be penalized in some way. This sends a message to the athlete that their training is more important than their life outside. Things that happen are often out of their control and may actually be their parent's, or someone else's, fault. The funny thing is, if you make the experience good enough, and positive enough, the athletes will be the ones insisting they are on time. If these are the rules you are putting in place, you'll find that if athletes fear the possibility of punishment, especially younger kids, they will just not want to come to training. Be invested in your athlete's lives, ask them why they were late and sympathize with them, because they're probably already disappointed that they were late for class.

Number 2: Help athletes succeed

Even though we should think of our athletes as people first, as their coach we still want to help them achieve everything they can in the sport. From my experience this is the part of coaching that everyone is already on board with and doing very well. Coaches educate themselves, understand the development pathways, foster skill learning, enter competitions at the correct level and they generally do everything that they can to help the athletes they coach to achieve skills. The important thing to remember is that this is number two of the most important things a coach can do. There needs to be a balance where coaches help the athlete reach their potential, without forcing skill development as the only or main goal.

When someone signs up for a sport, especially gymnastics, they do so because they want to. They want to be the best they can, they want to do well at competitions, they want to train hard. This motivation is already within them. So, our job as a coach should be to help them, not force them. I honestly believe that a coach should never have to 'motivate' an athlete through yelling, ultimatums or punishments. Instead we should be giving them the tools they both want and need to achieve their best and continue to foster their self-motivation within. The coach's goal is to both educate athletes to gain skills, but also to support and empathize with them when things get tough.

Number 3: Have Fun

Have you ever played an active game like tag, or a social basketball game with friends, only to realize how exhausted you are after you stop? That's because when you're having fun you forget that you're working hard, and you just keep going. This is a far more effective way to motivate, engage and teach your athletes, rather than applying an action and consequence method. It is also a much easier and more fun way for you as a coach.

Whenever you achieve something, especially in a game or fun environment, your brain releases a chemical called dopamine. This chemical is addicting and responsible for making you feel good. Whenever an athlete gets this feeling, they will want to push themselves to achieve more. Dr Martha Burns, a neuroscientist and leading expert on how children learn, calls dopamine the "save button." When dopamine is present during an event or experience, we remember it. But when it's absent, nothing seems to stick. The more interested we are in an activity; the more dopamine is released and the better we remember it.

Once we understand that our role as a coach is to help people have better lives and create a fun environment, we are one step closer to developing better athletes. They will be better at their sport, easier to coach and better at life. Who knows what they will achieve in their life when we understand this incredible opportunity we have as coaches to develop so much more than just skills?

3 WHAT IS SUCCESS

Before we can help our athletes achieve success it is important to understand exactly what we believe success is. I want you to take a moment to think about yourself as a coach, thinking both about the athletes you coach and the environment you coach in. I am asking you to get yourself into your coaching headspace. Once you're there, read the following Oxford Dictionary definition of success in the context of coaching.

Success: "The accomplishment of an aim or purpose."

When you read that, did you think about your own 'aim or purpose' or the 'aim or purpose' of your athletes? If you thought of your own aim or purpose, then what about your athlete? The coach is first and foremost there for the athletes and this mindset should be priority one. Your goal should be to continually improve your coaching in order to help your athletes be the best they can be. Finding the balance between the success of your athletes and the success in your own career is paramount. Focusing primarily on the athletes you coach and finding the tools you need to achieve success for them will inevitably lead to your coaching success too.

One of the hardest parts of trying to help your athletes succeed is recognizing that success looks different to every individual. Some athletes are destined for the world stage while others will be more than fulfilled by winning a local competition or game. Sometimes, an athlete can feel successful when they simply make a new friend.

So how do we help everyone succeed when it can look so dramatically different for each individual? The first step is to understand exactly what success looks like for each athlete that you are coaching. The obvious thing to do is ask them what success means to them. You should definitely do this first; however, they will often be unsure, or they will think they know, but really are only saying what they think you want to hear. This is surprisingly common in athletes who just want to please their coach.

Goal setting programs are a good tactic to establish athletic success. Goals enable the athlete to think about and set their own individual levels of achievement. There are many resources out there to help with goal setting and I encourage you to look through some of them. A simple google search using the term 'Goal

Setting' will return numerous helpful websites, books, videos and more to help you set something up. A great recourse that helps turn big goals in to achievable steps is an application called "Goalscape". Although I no longer use the app, I continue to use some of the principles I learned going through the process.

The most effective way of understanding anyone's goals, or vision of success, is to get to know them individually. Think of someone close to you, your partner, best friend or a close relative, do you know what success looks like to them? When I think of my wife, I can tell you success for her is helping people she comes across in her life. She feels like she has achieved something good if someone is going through a tough time and she helps them get through it. Every day she does little things, in all her interactions, that tell me this is what she strives for. I see it in the way she parents our children, the way she talks to her friends and the way she supports me. I know this because I have taken the time to learn about her and have seen and taken note of the things that make her happy. I will double check this idea of success with her before I publish this book, but I feel I know her so well that even though she's never actually articulated this to me, I think it will be true. Note: I checked, and I was correct *phew.

Getting to know your athletes is so important that you should be constantly looking for ways to learn more during your time with them. I recommend using a bookmark, or taking some notes on the following tips, so you can refer to these as you get to know your athletes better.

Stage 1: Names

The first stage of knowing your athletes is to know their names. This may seem obvious, but I think it's great to go a little further and not only find out their names, but also the names of those close to them. I do it in this order: find out their names (first and last), their parents or guardians names, their siblings, their pets and their best friend(s). This is helpful to begin with because you can then identify your athlete easily and positively interact with their families when you know all their names too. It can take a long time to remember so many names, which I personally need to put a lot of effort into, but the rewards are certainly worth it. My tactic is to play regular guessing games. During warmups I go up to each athlete and try and guess their parent's names asking them to correct me when I get it wrong. I do this over and over and over until I have all the names right. This can take a while, sometimes up to a year, but it can spark some fantastic conversations along the way.

Stage 2: Family Career

The next step is to find out what their parents do for a job and if they are old enough, what your athlete does. It can also be fun to talk about what they want to do when they're older. Once again, my process for trying to get to know this information is to simply ask the athletes over and over until I remember. I wouldn't say you need to memorize all this information, but it certainly doesn't hurt to try. Knowing an athlete's family can give invaluable insights and provide extremely valuable additional information that will help your coaching. Establishing information like, do they have ambitious parents, do they have parents who value happiness over money, do they have parents in caring careers, are their parents together or separated or do they work all the time can help you understand the environment your athlete has outside of training. It also helps to understand the contribution all of this has to shaping their future and their performance as an athlete.

When you coach an athlete, the family of that athlete is putting their trust in you and showing that you care enough to get to know the whole family gives the parents a great impression of you. Humans absolutely love it when others show interest in them. If you can approach parents/guardians knowing their name and starting a conversation about their career or some other detail, you help create a team between you and them. This will help build important trust and will be a resource for you if you need help with challenges associated with coaching that athlete. Who better than their family to help you understand how an athlete gets through tough times?

Stage 3: Athlete's Interests

Learning all about your athlete's interests is important when getting to know them well. Stage three is all knowledge on a deeper level. If you listen and observe carefully, you will learn everything you ever need to know about each individual in order to help understand their goals and help them succeed. Here's some examples. What kind of things do they do in their spare time? Do they play another sport? What are they like at school? What subjects do they study (if any)?

The only real way to find this out is through organic conversation, so it's important to create time for this. I use our warmup time, again, to go around and talk to each individual and always start with "How was your day?". I often get simple responses like "good" or "not bad" but sometimes I learn something about what they did that sparks conversation. Recently asking this question I learned that one of my gymnasts sat a test to determine whether she would get a full scholarship at one of the best schools in the area. This led me to ask questions about her study regime and how she organized her time. I learned from this conversation that she was very list orientated and from that I was able to adjust her program to include very specific lists for each section of training. The long-term result of that one conversation was a ten-fold increase in her motivation levels.

Another tactic that I've used over the years, is to allocate ten minutes in training to talk to athletes about their lives outside of sporting interests. I have the athletes stand in a circle and ask them to list three non-gymnastics interests that they have. I usually begin to help set the tone and say something like, my three interests are off-roading, playing guitar and trying new things. The last time I did this, I found out that six of my eight gymnasts liked spontaneous activity. I was able to introduce a mix up session in the training program every now and then, which had a very positive response. I replaced planned programs with a fun but beneficial game or something similar. This specifically helped increase motivation that resulted in enhanced training sessions and it all came from a group chat identifying the athlete's interests. If you are in tune with your athletes you will naturally get to know them well, which will have several benefits.

So how do we use this information to figure out what success means to them? What you'll find, or may have found already, is that the more you know your athletes the more likely you are to know what they want to achieve. Once you know the athletes you are coaching well, you can help them see what success truly means for each of them. For example, I currently have some gymnasts who are doing very well in their current stream and I suspected they would like a further challenge to gain new and harder skills in the future. To confirm this, I asked them how they felt about their current stream. Their responses were very positive but both articulated that they would be interested in something more challenging. We are now looking to advance them for next year. Had I just guessed this and not asked for their input it could have been a totally different story. Have you ever been told to do something without being asked for your opinion first? It never feels good. Let's say these athletes turn up to the first competition in their new level and don't perform well. If they were just told to advance, without any input, they may now resent me as their coach and possibly think they aren't actually good enough. Their input means they will take ownership over the decision and use that to motivate them to do better. This is an 'I chose this, so I have to make it work' approach that is more powerful than having a coach simply tell them they are ready.

I once again gained further insight into this through my survey. I discovered that less than 10% of gymnasts are motivated to train hard by external factors (e.g. their coach, parents etc.) and over 80% are motivated internally, with 54% being motivated by the love for their sport. When it came to competitive success, 11% were motivated by their parent or a coach, with 27% loving the feeling of success and another 27% wanting to prove it to themselves. This really shows me that as a coach, dictating things to your gymnasts like moving to competitive levels, changing streams and deciding training programs without their input, is likely to result in more failure than success. Athletes are not motivated by you or anyone else, they are motivated by their own internal drive, and if you really want success for your athletes you will need them to give significant input into how they are coached. Everyone's measure of success is not only different, but it can also change from day to day. One day an athlete can believe they are going to the Olympics, the next day they're thinking of trying another sport. As a coach, you will be far more effective knowing your athletes well first, giving you a much better chance of deeply understanding them and helping them discover their goals organically.

For those that believe success primarily includes outstanding performance and competitive success, let's examine that a bit more. What exactly does someone need to achieve competitive success? Let's look at what the best of the best has to say.

"Never say never because limits, like fears, are often just illusions" – Michael Jordan

"I hated every minute of training. But I said, Don't Quit. Suffer now and live the rest of your life a champion" – Mohammad Ali

"I don't run away from a challenge because I am afraid. Instead, I run towards it because the only way to escape fear is to trample it beneath your feet" – Nadia Comaneci

It is overwhelmingly clear that success is less about skill and technique, and more about determination, self-belief and other "soft" qualities. This is something to always remember when coaching athletes. The skills that you teach them, apart from the sport specific ones, don't always seem tangible but are extremely important if you are serious about helping them to succeed in life. So many times, I have seen coaches forcing hard work on their athletes, threatening punishment, yelling and using emotional blackmail, but none of these techniques will ever lead to great motivation, determination or hard work. They are instead short-term methods that will deliver short term results. In fact, the only long-term effects could be emotionally detrimental. To achieve lasting success both at training and beyond, we should review how we coach our athletes and aim to inspire them to succeed in every single little or big interaction we have.

4 HOW ATHLETES DEFINE THEMSELVES

I want you to take a moment and think about a sport that you did when you were younger. If you didn't do a sport, think about something you did that involved a coach, mentor or even a classroom teacher. Now, I want you to think about when you were with that person, try to remember the most common things they told you. Once you can remember that, think about how that made you feel.

Whether what you thought about in this little exercise was positive or negative, I'm confident that whatever you thought about contributed to who you are as a person today. If you thought hard about your previous experiences, I'm sure you could find thousands of examples of the little things you were told along the way, that have helped define who you are today. This example encapsulates the power you have as a coach. The things you say create experiences for these athletes, which can and will shape their lives. As a comic book fan, I can't help but think of Uncle Ben in Spider-Man, "With great power comes great responsibility" and that is exactly why we need to care deeply about what we are saying as coaches, mentors and friends. We need to be planned and intentional about the words we use and the effect they will have on those we are speaking to.

When I trained as a gymnast, there was a boy called Dillan who was not very flexible. Every time we warmed up our coach would say "Dillan start stretching". He would respond every time with "I am stretching". When he spoke to others about gymnastics he would say "it's fun, but I can't stretch so I'm not very good." This example highlights how an athlete defined themselves based on what their coach was telling them. In conversation with these ex gymnasts I have mentioned throughout the book so far, I asked them what they remembered most about the coaching they received. One girl hadn't trained in over 5 years and her response was "I always bent my legs, so my coach always said, "straighten your legs". Not only was it clear that her coach had told her this over and over, but she continued to tell me she wasn't that good at gymnastics because she couldn't straighten her legs. When quizzed further, she still says that she was the gymnast with the bendy legs. This girl's whole perception of herself as a gymnast has been defined by what her coach chose to highlight to her over and over again, and unfortunately for her, this was something negative. There really is so much power in what we say.

Have you ever worn a new item of clothing, maybe a new sweater, and been told by multiple people how nice it looks on you? Does that make you want to wear it more or less? The reality is we believe what people tell us, and it's the opinions of those closest to us that we value the highest. If you've ever done a sport to a reasonable level, you will have to agree that it's your coach and the people you train with every day, whose opinions matter the most. Those opinions have the power to define how others see you and how you define yourself.

So, what can we do as coaches to help people define themselves in a positive way? The first step is to think through everything you say to the athletes' you coach. It's important to consider how your words may be taken personally and can be interpreted in many ways. By framing what you say in positive ways can help increase an athlete's self-esteem. For example, if you continually tell someone to straighten their legs, they could define themselves as a 'bent leg gymnast'. If you tell someone to work hard, they could define themselves as 'lazy'. Feedback of this nature can be used at times to motivate people to train hard, but I'm suggesting you take a moment to understand that the things you say, and more particularly the words you use, can be interpreted in all sorts of ways especially if they are constantly repeated. You can be intentional about positively shaping others self-definition and self-esteem by consciously choosing the words you use. It can also be useful to reflect on whether your conversations with your athletes mostly end with them smiling and feeling uplifted or bowing their head with a slumped body language. This will usually give you an indication on how you're making your athletes feel.

Let's go back to Dillan for a moment. He was always told to stretch more, stretch harder etc. and he defined himself as a non-flexible gymnast. If, in his case, he was instead told more about his amazing straight legs during his floor tumbling, or somewhere else where his legs were straight, it is highly likely that he would think of himself as gymnast with straight legs. He still may not be particularly flexible, but if he had constant feedback that he had straight legs, he may think about that first and his focus might be on straight legs as those were the words he is constantly hearing. The positive feedback would more likely motivate him to train harder and work on his weaknesses, because he likely already knows his flexibility needs work.

Psychological testing has shown that positive people lead better, happier lives than the average. Optimism is a skill we can learn and as coaches, mentors, teachers, friends it is easy to use the positive to effect successful training outcomes and help athletes get the most from their sporting experiences.

5 POSITIVE FEEDBACK

As a coach you can help your athletes be the best version of themselves. This is a massive responsibility and it is extremely important it is taken seriously. When you take responsibility for something it's more than just trying your best, it's also about being accountable for what could go wrong as well. I have seen many coaches happy to take responsibility for the good things to come to their athletes, but then blame the bad stuff that happens on something or someone else. To take true responsibility for coaching and to be a positive influence, you must be willing to regularly look at what negative affects you could be having on an athlete's life. Once you accept that you, like everyone, has faults, then you can find ways to adjust and improve your coaching methods to ensure you have a positive, wholistic influence on the athlete.

Feedback is our greatest tool in helping athletes get

better at their sport. Our job is to teach them through regular feedback, so they understand what to focus on to improve. This happens repeatedly on any given training session. As a General Manager of a gymnastics club, I get to see a whole range of coaching, from preschoolers to elite level. On average our coaches give 42 pieces of feedback in 30 minutes and this is how I usually see it played out.

1. Coach explains, demonstrates or assigns a skill
2. Gymnasts perform the skill
3. Coach provides feedback
4. Gymnasts reattempts skill
5. Repeat from Step 2

Usually a coach is needing to split their attention between coaching multiple people and therefore athletes don't usually get feedback on every skill they perform. Athletes will however continue to practice skills over and over based on what feedback they have been given. This makes the importance of what we say and how we say it paramount.

As I've mentioned, an athlete will use their coach's words, not only to improve a skill, but also to help define themselves. They take on board what is said to them on many different levels. Regular positive feedback improves skill level, grows self-esteem and contributes to a great experience. In general, the coaching community agrees that delivering feedback in a positive way is more powerful than other coaching methods. There are currently two common methods taught to coaches to deliver positive feedback.

Feedback Sandwich

A feedback sandwich is the method of delivering constructive criticism in between two positive comments, for example: "That was a great forward roll, tuck your head in then it will be amazing!" For years this has been regarded as the best practice to deliver positive feedback.

I disagree.

Imagine you're catching up with a friend and they greet you with the following, "You look so good today, if you wore more make up you would look so much better, but I love your hair." Is that a positive comment? Does it leave you thinking you look good? Or does a comment like that only make you focus on the 'if you wore more makeup you would look better' bit, and really leave you wondering if the person thinks you look good at all? The reality is people are way too smart to fall for a feedback sandwich and will most likely just focus on the criticism or feedback in the middle. Before you think only adults would be aware of what's being said, you should meet my 4-year-old daughter…

Focus on the positive change

The other method commonly used to deliver positive feedback is to deliver it in a way that makes athletes focus on what is considered the 'right way to think'. I do agree with this one, sort of. The theory is your mind will always focus on what you are being told. For example, if I tell you not to imagine a pink elephant in a polka dot bikini it is very hard not to imagine exactly that. The same theory applies for coaching, if you ask an athlete not to bend their legs, they will struggle to keep their legs straight because what they have heard is 'bent legs'. Good coaches deliver positive feedback based on what their athletes should focus on, for example "keep your legs straight".

But….

Like the first method, this one has major flaws. Imagine another social setting where you are wearing a blue T-Shirt and your friend says, "you look better in red". Does that feel like a positive comment? Most likely your assumption is you don't look good in blue. Likewise, with athletes, when you give them feedback in this way, they can assume that they are doing it wrong and that contributes to how they define themselves. Remember that ex-gymnast who defined themselves as the bent leg gymnast because she remembers always being told to straighten her legs? She still remembers the feedback given to her and this has contributed to how she will define herself forever. She has a powerful lasting memory of negative feedback which has left a less than positive view, in part, of her time in gymnastics.

When an athlete is constantly told to do something, like straighten their legs, and they try to make that change only to still be told continually to straighten their legs, it's most likely they will just feel they can't do it. I coached a gymnast for over eight years who was extremely talented but lacked power in her floor tumbling and on the vault. I couldn't even count how many times during a training session, I would ask her to run faster. Since her retirement I've had multiple conversations with her, and she admits that this frustrated her and made her feel like a slow runner. In her mind she was running as fast as she could and was being punished for being slow. In my mind I had thought she could run faster and felt she improved every time I reminded her. I assumed she was struggling to just push herself harder. This constant feedback, although framed positively, left her feeling like she would never be fast enough to do the vaults she wanted to do. She had ended up defining herself as a slow runner, even though she wasn't. As a result, every time she vaulted, she would run slow. This was not because she couldn't go faster but because her subconscious now believed she was slow and caused this to be evident in her performance. The feedback, that I so genuinely gave thinking it would help, was the very thing that made her worse.

So, what should we do? It's simple really, give **positive** feedback.

I'm not talking about the positively framed feedback or the fluffy 'good job' kind of feedback, I'm talking about telling your athletes what they do well. Spend your time looking out for what they are good at and telling them about it. For the gymnast with bent legs, try telling her when she is practicing her leaps what she is actually really doing well. Saying something like "wow, those leaps are so high" can make a difference to straight legs. Striving for higher leaps will naturally lead to straighter legs without using "your legs are bent, straighten them" type feedback. For my gymnast who struggled to run fast, positive feedback like "your stride technique is amazing" would have naturally helped her to get faster. She'd focus on her stride technique, making sure to keep doing it well, which directly results in a fast pace run. Imagine if every time she ran down that vault run; she was told something that she did well. I could have focused on her arms while she was running and told her they were always perfectly aligned for her run (which for the record, they were). Now suddenly she starts defining herself as the runner with good technique, and her subconscious of course will start working for her instead of against her. Imagine again the social situation where you wore the blue shirt. If you are just told that you look good in that T-Shirt, are you now not more likely to wear it again? Probably and quite likely any blue shirt for that matter.

Graham Kaufmann is the Senior Vice President of Coaching and Facilitation at Horn, a business coaching and consulting organisation. I recently stumbled across a video showing how he gives positive feedback. He identifies two types of feedback, there's 'OK Feedback' using words like 'Wow', 'Good Job' or 'That was great.' Then there's 'Fantastic Feedback' which Graham describes this way.

Circumstance.
What was the exact moment where you saw the thing you are providing feedback on? It is extremely important to be specific. Which exact skill was being performed and which specific part of the skill are you looking at? When you are giving feedback, this precise identification, not only helps the athlete understand exactly what you are talking about but also helps your credibility when giving the feedback. Rather than just

saying "you had straight legs" you would be able to say, "you had straight legs in your second leap." This makes feedback much more believable and easier to understand.

Choice.

"Of all the things you could do in that moment, you chose to do that." Making this sort of comment, particularly to gymnasts is important to consider. It is a general comment which has no specific reference to skill improvement. There's so much happening in any one skill that is performed, that it's important to focus on what part of the skill the gymnast has control over and is doing well. This provides an opportunity to tell them how good it was that they chose to do that skill the way they did, which leads to overall skill improvement. By understanding they are doing one part of the skill well, they become focused on another part they want to improve.

Consequence.

Feedback can be taken to a whole new level when a consequence is associated with that feedback being take on board. In gymnastics we can use scores, "because you have straight legs you can score 0.3 higher in your floor routine". The use of consequence will help your athletes realize the importance of the improvements they make, not only making them feel good but also making them more likely to continue making improvements. In my opinion, the best kind of consequences are when they are outlined in feedback that is individual and personal. The thing I am always telling my gymnasts, which is true by the way, is that I absolutely love gymnastics and I enjoy watching it.

When they perform a skill well, then I honestly get enjoyment out of it and I tell them that I do. This has a profound effect on the likelihood of them wanting to continue performing at the same or better level. This is another example demonstrating the power a coach has to influence their athletes.

It has been proven that when receiving negative feedback, the human brain activates its sympathetic nervous system, known as your 'Fight or Flight' system. When activated this dulls all our other senses to protect us from what's happening and enables focus on the 'danger' we perceive. When a coach gives a negative piece of feedback, they take away an athlete's ability to focus on anything except that negative. They are working out whether to fight or run away. This can mean that everything else you are trying to achieve as their coach can suffer, and often there's then no way of fixing the skill error. Research has also shown that positive recognition activates your parasympathetic nervous system, also known as a 'rest and digest' response. When this part of our nervous system is active, we feel a sense of wellbeing and our brains are primed and ready to learn. Science has constantly been proving that giving people praise and positive feedback, is significantly more likely to build new neural pathways that allows faster learning than negative feedback will ever be able to do.

Another great thing about focusing on the positive things, is it so much more fun for you as a coach. Instead of watching all the time for what your athletes are doing wrong, you get to watch out for what they are doing right. This is a much better headspace to be in as a coach and will keep you in a more positive state which is better for you and all of those around you. I genuinely love looking for things that people do well and making sure they know about it.

In my survey, one of the questions was 'Give a percentage estimate of how much of the feedback you received from your coach, was things that you already knew'. The average response was 61%. Two thirds of what coaches were telling these gymnasts were things they already knew. This makes total sense. Think about yourself. When people pick up on things you do wrong, do you already know about it? I know I do most of the time, and I find myself getting annoyed when people tell me about it. So, if your gymnasts already know most of what you are saying as a coach, why not find those specific positives and focus on them? Have you ever been told something positive about yourself? Unlike when you are being told over and over about something you are doing wrong and feeling so frustrated that you already know that, when you are told about good things over and over, it simply makes you feel better about yourself and more motivated to do more. It comes back to nurturing that inner motivation your athletes have within them, they wouldn't be there if they didn't want to improve, they're already battling themselves to improve. The positive attention is really what athletes, and all of us, crave.

I recently watched an elite development program of ten gymnasts aged between nine and eleven years old. These were a group of incredibly talented gymnasts for their age and had been selected into their program.

When I watched them train, I was absolutely blown away by how amazing they were. Yes, they have a way to go if they want to achieve big dreams and high-level success, but to me they were just mind blowingly good at gymnastics. As I watched them train, I counted how much feedback they were given by their coach. In thirty minutes, they were given sixty-one pieces of feedback, roughly six per gymnast in the group, each piece focusing on what needed to be fixed. Not once were they told they were doing any part of any skill correctly. They were only told what to do better. Now applying those statistics to their whole training session, given they train fifteen hours a week, fifty weeks a year, means they will be told nine thousand things they need to get better at. Nine thousand times where they will, most likely, feel they are not quite good enough for their coach. Nine thousand times where they might feel they will never be good enough to achieve their dreams, NINE THOUSAND! And not once told a specific thing they were good at. The craziest thing to me is that these kids are nine to eleven years old. Surely, they should absolutely feel good about themselves and the things they are doing so well. They are already so darn good at their sport that the development of a positive mindset could propel them to the very top.

If there is one thing you take away from reading this book, please let it be this. Give positive and specific feedback to your athletes as much as you can. You will see tremendous changes in the way they train, in their outlook and within yourself, changes that you probably never thought possible.

6 THE IMPORTANCE OF FEEDBACK

It has been widely accepted that there is value in using positive feedback in coaching, you've probably heard the popular phrase 'catch people doing the right thing'. Some people question however if this can really help an athlete understand what they need to do to improve. Can they really learn just by being told what they're doing well? The short answer is yes. Even by solely focusing on what your athlete is doing well, they are still likely to continue to learn and develop, not only their strengths, but make improvements and learn new skills too. I would argue that they are more likely to learn faster when their coach only focuses on the positives than only, or even partly, focusing on the negatives. I understand that some coaches won't be able to adapt to a positive only style of coaching, and for them to find a balance I recommend using a 4:1 ratio method. That is, 4 positive pieces of feedback to

1 piece of constructive criticism, we will discuss this further later on. First, let's look at the importance of constructive feedback and how we can deliver it in the best possible way.

When we are delivering commentary on training skill errors, we need to be specific and clear about what we are saying to our athletes. Generalised feedback will not get results and instead risk confusion. For example, you are teaching a gymnast a front sault on floor. A skill where a gymnast runs on the floor, jumps off two feet, flips over forward and lands back on their feet. You know the gymnast needs to go higher. Simply telling them to go higher is not likely to result in any change. If they've stumbled or landed on their bottom instead of their feet, they're likely to already know they need to go higher. As an alternative, when you are coaching you can look at the reason they aren't going high and work on fixing the specifics. There is real value in being knowledgeable enough about your sport, to be able to identify the specifics of a skill that needs fixing and taking the time to think and know about each component of the skill. Once you have done that then it's about communicating your knowledge to achieve skill correction and improvement. I know my gymnast isn't getting high enough in their front sault because they're losing power jumping too high in their take off. This is pushing momentum down into the ground rather than it lifting them higher into the air. They will have greater success in improving their skills if I explain this and give them ways to fix their jump in take-off.

Focusing on skill specifics that need to be fixed is

the key. There's no point asking an athlete to change one thing if there are lead up skills that need fixing first. A swing pullover is a skill on bars where a gymnast swings under the bar, then kicks over the bar finishing on top with their hips on the bar. There would be no point asking a gymnast performing a pullover to straighten their legs (which is mostly just aesthetically pleasing), if their swings weren't big enough or they weren't initiating the skill at the correct time prior to focusing on straight legs. Most coaches, when they take the time, know specifically what to focus on when they are trying to fix a skill. Sometimes it seems easier to just suggest general corrections, but I guarantee your athletes will respond better when they're coach gives positive, relevant and informed feedback.

The right things to focus on varies between athletes. What works for Joe won't always work for Suzy. It is important for a coach to make sure they individually understand their athletes. Knowing them well, as described in Chapter Two, provides a tool to help improve our own memory. Training your mind to know your athletes well will help you remember their skills and abilities. When you know your athletes holistically, you are better prepared for the times when things aren't working, and more likely to know the right avenue to help change things. Patience can be one of the hardest things a coach has to learn. When coaches aren't driven by a desire to put their athlete first, they tend to be impatient and rely on coaching methods that they've used before, rather than looking for individual solutions that are based on the athletes own learning style. I have found that knowing your athletes well and coaching with patience and empathy is exactly what will achieve amazing training results.

Mary-Anne Monckton, an Australian Commonwealth Games medalist in gymnastics, once said to me "When my gymnasts don't change after I give them feedback I assume it's one of two things; either they don't understand the feedback I'm giving them or they are scared of the change". This has stuck with me and although it may not be as black and white as this, it certainly shows that Mary-Anne has a lot of empathy for the athletes. Opposed to this attitude, a more regular tendency for coaches is to shout the same piece of feedback over and over and when there aren't instant results, they punish their athlete for not listening. This style assumes the athletes don't really want your help. I personally choose to believe that all my gymnasts try their best and want to do their best. If they aren't making the changes I am asking, then I need to find out why and change what I'm doing in order to achieve the outcome I am looking for.

Knowing that your athletes already understand two thirds of the feedback you give, the most important thing you can do, as a coach, is to focus on what you know they are ready to change. An athlete should be ready both physically and emotionally to make changes you are asking of them, and if your feedback doesn't work then the best thing you can do is to change your approach.

When giving feedback, you should always try and focus on what can be controlled by your athlete and deliver it in a way that your athlete can understand. I recently learned this lesson again from a kinder gym coach. In order for a three-year-old to understand changes you want them to make in their gymnastics, you really must adjust how you communicate what needs correcting. This coach made a simple change on bars when trying to get participants to have straight arms. Instead of simply saying 'straighten your arms', which although logical is not usually interpreted properly by preschoolers, the coach asked them to push down on the bar and each gymnast immediately straightened their arms. This happened because the coach took the time to consider both the feeling and components of the skill that the children had to understand, in order to make the change. It worked much better than just focusing on the error of having bent arms. Small changes in the way we deliver our coaching instruction can make all the difference.

A great way to approach giving constructive feedback is to ask questions like, "What did you feel like you could do better?" When using this technique, I find that at least two out of three times the athlete will answer with exactly what they should be focusing on. They already know. It's good to follow up with, "So what are you going to do this time?". Again, they will more times than not, know the answer and this approach leads to changes being made. You will find your athletes are far more willing to take responsibility for their own skill development when you respect them enough to ask their opinion first. As they often know the answers and have good ideas, empowering your gymnast in this way can often fast track their improvement of a skill error.

The other important thing to remember, when trying to fix skill errors, is to make sure you take the time to explain why they need to fix that error. No matter what it is they are trying to fix, there is most likely a scientific and logical reason for the change. It really doesn't matter how complicated the reason either. It's as much about teaching athletes about the skills in their sport, as it is taking them on the journey of what each small skill correction means to the overall skill. To illustrate this point, in gymnastics, head position is something that is extremely important. That's because your proprioceptors in your inner ear are responsible for helping you know where you are in space. There are thousands of hair cells inside your inner ear that are stimulated by fluid. As the fluid moves around, based on gravity, the different hair cells send a message back to the brain to tell us where we are within the space we are using. In gymnastics, many skills have you flipping and twisting through the air, at a rate too fast for your eyes to register, so we rely heavily on this proprioception from the inner ear to position us. If your head is in the wrong position while you are in the air, it can throw the entire skill off leading to skill errors and even injury. I often find myself explaining this to gymnasts, even younger ones, to help them understand why they need to change their head position. When you simply correct a skill, without a detailed explanation, they can often tell themselves their way feels better and not feel the need to actually correct it. After all, they're not making that error because they want to do the skill badly, it's more likely they do it because it feels more natural or easier. It is so important to take the athletes you train on a journey with you by helping them to understand the complexities of skill development. This also makes an important contribution to their general knowledge and confidence.

Finding things that athletes are doing well and praising them for that is the most effective way to facilitate learning. Positive and constructive feedback primes the brain and enables athletes to be ready to strengthen and build more neural pathways. Positive feedback is so effective when it is given on its own that pairing it with a correction, or negative feedback, is just not necessary. So many times, I see coaches celebrating a positive change with an athlete, followed straight away with something to fix. Saying to your athlete, "Yay, you finally caught the high bar, now do it with straight legs" does not make them feel good. They are just left focusing on the "now fix this" and not on the celebration of what they have achieved. If their perception is that you always emphasize the next thing to fix, and there's no celebration for achievement, this is going to encourage a very negative head space. It is so powerful to take the time and be happy for the achievements along the way. The next skill fix can wait. Repeating the successful skill one more time before fixing the next error will reinforce the correction and instill a sense of achievement and success.

The word celebrate is important. You need to create a culture with your athletes where you are on their side and happy for them when they do good things. I'm not actually talking about performance here, or even learning new skills. The most important thing for you to celebrate is the tiny changes your athletes make, that you as a coach know will help them long term. If you feel it's important enough to give a correction or feedback on something, you should be extremely happy, proud and excited when your athlete is able to make that change. You can make a habit of celebrating the small changes they make, even if it's made the overall skill worse. If they made the change you asked for, that is a big deal. Do you think your athletes will be happy to change something else when your reaction from the last change has been so positive? Remember to celebrate without criticism, if you say "The skill was worse but at least you made the correction" the focus will be on the negative, that the skill was worse. I guarantee you; the athlete already knew the overall skill was worse and they will want to make it better too. As the coach you are the expert so celebrate each little win so you can work together to make the rest of the skill better as well.

Small celebrations not only change the way your athlete will think about corrections and making changes, it will also create a culture in your group where all the small changes made are the most important things at training. If you only celebrate the big achievements, like new skills and great performances, then the culture created is focused on that. In the long run, a hard-working athlete will usually beat a talented one, so celebrating the hard work and small changes all the time encourages hard work. Athletes should also be celebrated when they perform well and gain new skills, but the little wins are so important to the overall. In fact, it's likely that all the little things done well and celebrated deliver the big achievements. Highlight the fact that the reason they got that skill was because of all the hard work they did on those skill components, like strength or drills. Show your other athletes that they can achieve anything if they work hard on the little things and make the right changes moving forward and celebrate these things along the way.

I coach a group of four retired gymnasts who come in once or twice a week to do some light training and fitness. As an experiment, I recently decided to increase the strength program making it a little harder and then I started giving a lot of positive praise. It was amazing to see what happened when I gave specific praise. For example, I said to one of the girls "Your legs are so tight in that dish", suddenly the other three gymnasts in the group all tightened their legs as well. Giving praise to one athlete made the other athletes automatically want to receive the same praise. They tried harder and made the change too. The best thing about this was I told the group that I was going to implement the 'only positive feedback' method and even though they knew what I was up to they couldn't help but 'fall for it'.

As humans we crave attention. Although it's been proven that we prefer positive attention, we are also sub-consciously believe that negative attention is better than none. In 2009 the Gallup Institute ran a study on 1,003 US employees on engagement at work. They found that supervisors who focused their attention on employees' strengths and positive characteristics had only 1 in 100 employees actively disengaged. Supervisors who focused on weaknesses had 22% of their employees disengaged and supervisors who ignored their employees had 40% of them disengaged. This demonstrates how individuals will engage with negative feedback over no feedback, but positive feedback is drastically better in engaging people. If you are given negative feedback you are twice as likely to be engaged than if you get no feedback. If you get positive praise you are 20 times more likely to be engaged than if you get negative feedback, or 40 times more likely to be engaged than if you get no feedback. This is one of many studies that have shown strong evidence towards the power of positive feedback and the culture it can create amongst individuals.

The more you focus on the positive things that your athletes or gymnasts do, the better they will engage, and the more likely they will be to make changes to become better athletes. As a coach when you train your athletes to improve, you can experiment using the positive techniques discussed above. You will see how your athletes improve their skills faster and with greater quality. You will also show them that you respect them and will be empowering them to take responsibility for their own development.

7 THE 4:1 RATIO

Emily Heaphy and consultant Marcial Losada conducted research on team leaders to determine the best ratio of using positive feedback versus constructive criticism. The positive feedback included comments to team members letting them know what they did well and giving constructive criticism was telling them what they needed to improve. They had team leaders use different ratios of negative and positive comments with their teams and then the performance of those teams was measured and compared. They concluded that the ideal ratio, for optimum team performance, was 5.6 pieces of positive feedback to 1 constructive criticism. This research also showed that constructive criticism without positive comments lead to much lower performance. I personally decided to commit to a 4:1 ratio which I'll explain more a little later.

My experience tells me that humans are usually not very good at receiving praise. I personally find that when I compliment people with something like "that shirt looks great on you", I am often met with responses that are negative. For example, "Oh, it's just an old shirt", or worse, "I don't really like it". Rarely when giving a compliment do I find the other person just says thank you. In fact, I will admit I struggle to simply say thank you myself when given a compliment, without then adding a negative as well. I find myself saying things like "yes we are doing well but we have some more work to do". In contrast, when offered criticism, people believe it straight away and can find themselves lingering on the negative comment. This also triggers a response to do everything possible to avoid receiving similar comments in the future. For example, if your gymnast is only ever hearing faults in a particular skill, they'll likely just wait until you're watching someone else before they practice it to avoid you criticizing them. That is a crucial reason to make sure you are giving significantly more positive comments than negative, or even just constructive ones. Repeating the positives over and over will lead to faster self-belief pattern and greater success.

Self-confidence is extremely important to success. If an athlete doesn't have confidence, they will be having negative thoughts, and as you likely know, self-talk is extremely powerful. If someone believes they are not good enough, they are not very likely to be, good enough. It becomes a self-fulfilling prophesy. No matter how confident someone seems on the outside, they will still need constant validation that they are good enough to truly believe in themselves. As coaches, if we want our athletes to have confidence, the best thing we can do is constantly tell them they are good enough. The best way to do that is to praise them through specific positive comments that the individual needs to hear. Tell them exactly what it was they did well, where they did it, the choices they made, what happened or could happen because of the choices they're making. Positive feedback is needed repeatedly and significantly more often than negative or constructive comments to install success. The more negative things you say, the more you will simply undermine any positive comments you've made.

Finding specific, individually appropriate ways to praise each athlete will always be received well. This positive outlook will have powerful and long-lasting impact, not only for the athlete but for you as a coach as well.

I am proud of you. Probably the five most powerful words you could ever say, you may not realize it but the athletes you coach actually want to please you. They want to train, they want to do the right thing, they want to get better and they want your approval. Sometimes even more than they want their parent's attention. The power that the words "I am proud of you" can have is amazing. Used after an athlete makes a correction, gets a new skill or makes any improvement will have a positive impact on performance. Give it a go when you're coaching next and see the reaction you get. But more importantly "I am proud of you" is a tool that can help your athletes through tough times. Letting someone know that you are proud of them, even if they underperform, gives hope and comfort and leads to motivation to improve, rather than despair. I cannot stress enough the importance of responding this way compared to pointing out your athletes' failings. This is the exact moment you have the power to build an individual up, or completely tear them down. This is also the exact moment where negative coaches cause the kind of emotional impact that leads to mental health issues in their gymnasts' long term.

I once had a gymnast who was competing at a competition in a level higher than she felt ready for, despite the number of times I assured her she was. At the competition she looked around and felt out of place. As is often the case with gymnastics, when gymnasts mentally tear themselves down, she had a couple of falls and did not perform as well as she would have liked. When I spoke to her, she expressed that she felt embarrassed because she didn't belong there. This broke my heart. I do what I do to make people happy, not for them to feel like this. My response was to tell her how proud I was, then I stood up and with a loud voice exclaimed "This is my gymnast", so everyone could hear. I knew my gymnast; I knew that all she really wanted was for someone to accept her and be proud of her. Of course, this action alone didn't completely solve her issues and she wasn't magically 100% happy again, but she did improve. She even went on to work harder in training and smashed the next competition out of the park. I think this experience was one that truly taught me the power of your words and actions. That you are proud of your athlete is one of the greatest, and most sincere, tools you can use as a coach.

Another powerful belief you can share with your athlete is trust. Personally, being told the words "I trust you" means a lot to me. Having people tell me the positive things they might think and feel, regularly, is a clear way I can feel their trust in me. When I am told that I'm doing something wrong it makes me feel undervalued, decreases my self-worth and shatters my confidence. My personal response to negative feedback is usually to feel defensive, get upset and question my worth in my position. I'm sure this isn't something anyone really wants to invoke in me, and it's certainly not a feeling I would want for my athletes. When you are constantly reminded of the good things you are doing and you feel a sense of worth from your coach or superior, it completely changes the way you can handle criticism. When you are confident that someone thinks good things of you, you are much more likely to take on constructive criticism for what it is and not let it be hurtful.

I currently have the privilege to oversee a team of eight managers, who I trust completely. This trust enabled me to leave the team to run the business, while I took ten weeks off to travel across the world and write this book. I constantly tell my team about all the great things they do and remind them of how proud I am, both as a team and individually. If something great happens I try my best to celebrate that with them and make sure they know how I feel. In fact, I would probably say my ratio of positive to constructive criticism with them is more like 20:1. I also make sure they are not just expected to take responsibility for their work, but that they are given real responsibility.

There is a difference. I don't just give them work to do and make sure they do it, I give them the responsibility as a leader to make their own decisions and take ownership of both achievements and mistakes.

As you can probably imagine, my team also make a point of being positive with their teams and use the 4:1 approach in their management. Managing business teams is not that different to coaching. The positive approach is so embedded in our culture that it is written into our policies. The opening line for our performance review policy is: Staff should be receiving feedback year-round at a ratio of 4 positive to 1 constructive criticism. If you wait until a review to bring something up it's usually too late.

At work we use an employee NPS or Net Promoter Score survey to measure staff satisfaction. NPS is a survey where you ask one question "How likely are you to recommend here as a place to work?" Employees are asked to rate on a scale of 1-10. Responses numbered 9 & 10 are classified as promoters, 7 & 8 are classified as passives and 1-6 are classified as detractors. The percentage of detractors is then subtracted from the percentage of promoters to get the final NPS result. The NPS is used internationally to measure both employee satisfaction and customer satisfaction. On our most recent survey we scored 61 on the employee NPS. According to Forbes magazine, Google is the second-best place in the world to work and they scored 40 on their most recent NPS. I guess this shows we must be the best place in the world to work!

Positive feedback for staff is not the only thing that contributes to workplace satisfaction, but I firmly believe that making sure we regularly praise our people is one of the greatest contributions to our happy team. Everyone is engaged, happy to work hard and most of all feel like they belong, and this is because they are regularly praised for the good things they are doing.

So why 4:1 and not 5.6:1. There is no scientific or research backed reason to choose 4:1 over other ratio's, but to be honest, I chose 4:1 because I find it works so well in a practical sense. When I discovered the research that identified the best ratio is 5.6:1, I wanted to change the way I was coaching and get as close to this number as I could. So, I wondered how I was going to make sure that each one of my gymnasts got a ratio of 5.6 positive comments to every 1 error correction. With a group of eight gymnasts the 5.6-1 ratio felt impossible to track for everyone. As a first step I started to track all my comments and make sure I was getting close to hitting the ratio. Over time I would have to trust that the ratio would work out for everyone. The next thing I tried was to buy two counters, that you click with your thumb, to count the comments I made while coaching but that was laborious, so logic prevailed and I started to use a method of counting on my fingers. I started counting the number of times I gave praise on my left hand while I was coaching. I deliberately chose my left hand because it meant my right hand was free for my crazy arm waves that I tend to do while coaching. I quickly realized that the ratio would need to be 5:1 since I only have 5 fingers. I began counting 5 praise points on my left hand, every time I got to 5, I would then allow myself to give a correction before starting over again. The difficulty I ran into, was having all 5 fingers open while coaching was the same as relaxing my hand. I would often have given five positive comments and then couldn't remember if I had given a correction, or if I had accidently, given too many corrections. I was still in default mode to give corrections rather than lots of positive feedback. After all that trial and error, I tried using four fingers to count praise and then a thumbs up to count the error correction. This 4:1 ratio worked really well for me.

In the end, the point is to find a way of making sure that the times you offer positive feedback outweigh the times you give corrections or criticism. So, a ratio of 4:1, 5.6:1 or a similar ratio will give you the positive outcomes you're looking for. 4:1 has worked for me and it's what I now use every coaching session without needing mental effort to count what I'm saying.

I encourage you to try the 4:1 ratio approach next time you are coaching and see what happens. From the moment I started using it, I noticed a couple of things. Firstly, the gymnasts didn't really seem to consciously pick up any difference in my coaching. When I gave them praise, they looked at me and responded the same way as when I gave an error correction, except they had a big smile on their faces. The other thing I noticed; was they were fixing their errors faster. I honestly had my doubts at first that they were going to learn enough without me constantly correcting them. They certainly did. They responded extremely well, they were working harder, listening better and making fewer errors. To me this was all the proof I needed, and I am now converted to the 4:1 ratio for athlete feedback and hopefully you will be too.

8 ATMOSPHERE IS EVERYTHING

Have you ever read Simon Sinek's book, 'Start with Why'? This is one of my favourite books. It's not because I agree with everything he says, in fact I tend to disagree with some of his ideas, but because 'Start with Why' changed the way I think. It changed my ideas about decision making and the choices that define us every day. The book asks you to define your own personal 'why' statement, which is something that explains exactly what it is you are doing with your life. There is a lot more to the book than just this, and I recommend you read it, but for now here's what I worked out was my 'why'.

"I want to have a positive effect on people so they can then make the world a happier place."

Once I defined this, it really helped me in my everyday actions. Now I look at every personal interaction I have, as having either a positive or negative effect on others. I don't believe the chances of a "neutral" interaction are very high, if they exist at all, so every interaction I have is either a good or bad one. Why then wouldn't I aim for each of those interactions to be good? That is what I try to do every day. Even though as a manager of one hundred and eighty staff it is sometimes hard to achieve every single time. I keep coming back to my 'why' and it helps, even with the tough conversations I must have sometimes.

Whether you are like me and intentionally want to have a positive effect, or you just want to coach successful athletes, there is great value in positive interactions as the best way to get your desired outcome. This has a great influence on culture and atmosphere. It is applicable to the experience that individual athletes have with their coach. You are probably already aware that group culture is important, and you've probably seen the effect of a bad culture where athletes don't want to train, and you just can't seem to say or do anything to change that. You've probably also seen the opposite, when it's one of those days that everyone is on point, working hard and you don't have to try. I strive to be intentional about the culture I create and work hard to create positive interactions.

As a coach you are the leader of creating culture and even though sometimes it feels like you have no control, your daily actions repeated over time are exactly what sets expectations, feeling, atmosphere and builds experience. It's valuable to identify some of the mistake's coaches make when trying, consciously or sub-consciously, to set a training culture, so we can attempt to avoid them.

Inconsistency

It's important to know that no matter how good the culture is, there will always be days that are better than others. As a coach you need to try and level this out as much as possible. If as the leader you change from day to day, then why wouldn't your athletes expect they can change as well? If they have a good day and you are happy and praise them, but then on their bad days you get cranky, you are simply reaffirming that complete inconsistency is normal. In fact, your athletes will blame you for the training session whether you had anything to do with it or not. Instead if you intentionally stay happy on those bad days, maybe using a little less praise but overall staying positive, you're creating a reliable culture for your athletes. If you are consistent, then your athletes will realize that they need to take responsibility for a bad training session and own it. This helps the recognition that taking personal responsibility leads to improvement and can empower your athlete rather than discipline them.

Staying positive can be particularly hard if you are personally having a bad day before coaching. A few things I avoid when I am struggling to feel positive, is telling the athletes that I'm in a bad mood or correcting their behavior in that session. I still correct their skills of course but if behavior needs correcting, I always do this when I'm in the best mood. This way my actions are intentional, and I am not at risk of taking out my own emotions on the athletes. I have often seen coaches who deliberately focus on behavior when they are in a bad mood, probably because it provides personal release and helps them feel better, but at what expense? The athletes won't respond well to you expressing your negative emotion. If you want them to do well at their sport, and more importantly at life, then your bad mood and negative behavior will teach them the opposite. You risk them modeling your example and they will not do well at training or in their interactions with others. Those behaviors will never model the positive coaching influence that leads to athletic or personal growth.

Discipline

Have you ever been part of a group, perhaps a workplace or classroom, where you are reprimanded for your mistakes? How did it make you feel when you were told off or punished for your behavior? I know for me, it never felt good, and it certainly didn't motivate me to change. I've seen this kind of discipline used as a coaching tool many times, and I have been guilty of using it myself. You might have a particular behavior you expect for the group you're coaching, like silent warmups, time limits on programs, tardiness, and the list goes on, including any behaviors that you expect from your athletes with the intention that it will help them be better. However, if you give negative repercussions for athlete's behaviors you will only invoke fear, guaranteed. When scared, humans go into fight or flight mode. The fighters will stay, possibly even work harder, but their neurological system will be locked on the threat, which is the behavior they were punished for. They will then be unable to focus on other more important things. The people who take flight will simply avoid the situation that invoked the coach's negative reaction and try to avoid doing that again. I spoke to three gymnasts on separate occasions who admitted to me that they would not turn up to training if they were running late for fear of being told off. In that scenario, sure the coach has now created the desired culture, no one is late anymore, but at the expense that they've lost an athlete altogether because they're frightened of being late. Sometimes in an example like this a common phrase thrown around is, 'but that's what it takes, if they don't have what it takes, they just won't make it'. This is an incredibly out of date thought for any coach to have and does nothing but psychologically harm your athlete. For those gymnasts who do flight, and avoid, long term consequences can often mean these athletes desert the sport they may love.

As an alternative to the negative examples above, focusing on the behavior you want to see and not the behavior you don't want to see, will consistently deliver good results. When athletes are modeling good training behaviors, like working hard and arriving on time, celebrating them leads to repetition of positive behavior. I have seen this work successfully when reinforced through rewards given in point style systems, not that dissimilar to the house cup in Harry Potter. I have implemented a points system in my coaching programs for many years now and have seen many other gymnastics clubs doing the same. Generally, most coaches are happy with the results of a points system. Here is a simple model that works well. Split your athletes into teams or houses or some other form of group. Groups can be just the athletes you are coaching but it works better when a whole club or program are involved. Once groups have been established, each group achieves points for the behavior and hard work you want to see. Having some sort of ceremony or award at the end of an elected time period helps keep everyone motivated on the end goal. Points should be given by the coaches or selected coaches, and although there can be a rough overall guide, points should mostly be given at the coach's own discretion. The great thing about this is the athletes want the points, not for the prize or even the win, but because of the camaraderie this creates within the teams. No one wants to let their fellow housemates down.

There is a couple of traps to look out for and avoid in point systems.

Trap number 1: Listing ways to get points.

It's great to let everyone know what kind of things you are rewarding, hard work, no tardiness, support for friends, great listening, dedication to a new skill, etc. However, if you list them you can very quickly change the focus for your athletes. By creating a list, athletes now feel like they are entitled to each point that they receive, rather than being rewarded by their coach for individual achievements. When I think of the type of person I want my athletes to be, it generally doesn't involve entitlement. Another issue with a reward list is that you narrow the minds of your athletes to focusing only on those behaviors or values that are on the list. I would prefer to be open to have my athletes thrive in their own individual way and be able to reward them accordingly. In businesses too, I have often seen employee's waiver on performance, to focus on one key performance indicator that is linked to a bonus. This narrow focus limits the potential to find a wider variety of ways to reward great work. The same theory applies with points for athletes. A list style of allocating points means the same reward is given to each athlete regardless of the cost to them. This may be equal but not always equitable. For some athletes it's a lot harder to complete a task, maybe because they are less physically capable or for a whole variety of other possible reasons. It seems fair to me, rather than narrowing focus to a specific list of points, that individual achievements are better recognized. It may be possible to make a huge expansive list of achievements to have on a 'points list' but that sounds like a complicated system that would be impossible to understand.

Trap number 2: Taking points off.

I have already talked about the fight or flight system and how it is activated by punishing athletes. The same thing applies to having points removed. If points are taken off a group for behavior, now not only is it a punishment and fear provoker for individual athletes, you are also punishing their peers and friends. To the rest of the group, who have had points taken off, it feels just as bad for them. It feels unfair since they did nothing wrong. Have you ever received a group email from a superior reprimanding a behavior that happened, that you are sure you've never done? Or perhaps a meeting agenda point has been made about how we need to get better at a particular thing that you have no control over. Either way, if you are not guilty of what happened or haven't been part of the agenda item, then you sometimes second guess yourself or simply just feel really bad because you are being told off for something that someone else did. I have seen this often, in business and coaching, and it is disheartening. For group situations we should highlight the good being achieved and use praise in the public arena to celebrate with our peers. Criticism and corrections should be done one on one.

Reinforcing this, there is nothing better than random acts of appreciation. Whenever I do something, like the dishes at home, I do it because it's part of life, but there is no better feeling than having my wife thank me for doing it. Yet, like in many marriages, my wife and I often forget to do this for those everyday things. The same thing applies to coaching. We expect a certain level of commitment to training from our athletes and often forget to tell them how much we appreciate them for it. For them it's far from a mundane activity like doing the dishes, it's more likely something they pour their heart and soul into because it's their passion. Every small action an athlete does, that helps lead them to success, should be appreciated by their coach.

One of my favorite times of training is the lineup we do at the end of training. The gymnasts all line up so the coaching team can share some insights from the session and say goodbye. In the first part of the lineup, the gymnasts often share something about their training. I love this time because we always focus on the positives, even on bad days, so the gymnasts go home thinking of the good things they did in the session. I have found this helps motivate them to stick with it and encourages them to come back next time. But the real reason I love line up is because I get to share my insights from training. I take this role very seriously and think very hard about how the training session went and what people did well. I also make sure to thank them for those things. I am coaching a group of gymnasts who work very hard and are very supportive of each other, so luckily for me this part is always easy. I constantly remind them of how grateful I am to coach them, which is whole heartedly the truth, I know how important supporting each other is. When you are truthful and specific with your athletes, it will not only make them feel good, it will show them that what they do matters to you.

The most important thing about setting up a good culture in your team is to model the behaviors you want to see. Do you want everyone to be focused in warm up? Then you should be heavily involved in warm up, constantly giving praise to those focused in warm-up. If you disengage so will they. Maybe you want everyone to be early. If so, are you always the first one to arrive? If you're not, that's the first thing that needs to change. This approach doesn't always fix everything, but if you are not leading by example then everything else will end up failing. You are and always will be a role model and leader as a coach. If you take that responsibility seriously your athletes and you will both see the benefits, not only at training, but also in other areas of your lives.

9 FRIENDSHIP

At its core, gymnastics is an individual sport. Even at team events, you compete on your own and rely only on yourself for your standard of performance. This makes a team environment during training sessions even more important. In team sports, you rely on each other to pass the ball correctly, make the shot or run the correct play. The result of this is there is a natural reliance on each other. In gymnastics that doesn't occur at competitions, so to add the team element, we need to make sure it is a key component of training sessions.

So why is a team environment so important? One reason is oxytocin. Oxytocin is a neuropeptide, or hormone, that is released when we have meaningful relationships with friends and family. Oxytocin is often spoken of for its role in bonding mothers and babies or romantic relationships, but it also functions to make all social interactions feel good. It helps reduce anxiety and contributes to building trust in others. This means, an environment that initiates oxytocin release within your athletes, will lead to them feeling happier, calmer and create more positive relationships with one another. As a result, athletes will spend less time thinking negative thoughts about their peers, such as comparisons in skill or strength, and more time being happy for each other and doing what they came to do, train well.

I find it really important to provide a coaching environment that facilitates these relationships to grow. Athletes, especially gymnasts, need to understand the importance of relationships with one another, and that they're not in this alone. I always explain how having each other's backs, cheering each other on, helps them get the most out of their sport. It's important for them to understand they have support around them, which helps foster friendships but also empowers them individually and produces better athletes. I encourage these behaviors by rewarding and celebrating those who support and are kind to each other. I'm famous for 'wasting' time by having my athletes tell me jokes, but by doing this I create an atmosphere where it's ok to stop training for a moment in order to have a laugh and build relationships. My gymnasts then feel comfortable to also do this amongst themselves, not necessarily to tell jokes, but to build their friendships.

So many times, I see coaches punishing their gymnasts for talking amongst themselves and not really finding that balance between achieving outcomes and enjoying training. Athletes must train, and it can't all be social, however there are so many benefits to encouraging the social aspect of sport. When the balance is found you start to see an incredibly positive effect on your gymnast's achievements, but also watch them grow as people. In my conversations with retired gymnasts there was an obvious trend in their memories, that training was not all about how they were coached or their successes, but mostly about the friends they made. This is a great long-term goal we can have for our athletes, as friendships established in their sport can last a lifetime. The support of friends consistently has amazing benefit for their training and performance.

As humans we are naturally social beings, some people more so than others, but we all rely on the support of those around us to be the best we can. Nothing shows me the benefit of social connections more, than when athletes show excitement and drive for each other when achieving new skills. I can remember coaching a training session, after many like it before, where gymnasts were working towards a new skill called a back full. This is a full twisting back somersault in a stretched position. Five of the gymnasts in the group had already done all the progressions leading up to this skill and just needed to take that final step to complete the complicated skill. I reassured them that they were ready and said they could try it when they felt up to it. The gymnasts got together and discussed this as a group and agreed together that if one of them tried it, they all would. The first gymnast got up and the supportive cheers were deafening. The remaining five were so invested in their friend getting the skill and were whole heartedly behind her. Sure enough, off she goes and lands her first ever back full. One by one the remaining four gymnasts also got up, to similar cheers, and after each of them landed their skill there were celebrations to rival an Olympic win. All of this occurred without me needing to get involved. The key point here, is they were all supporting each other. There was also some healthy competition amongst them (if she gets it, I have to as well), but their main motivation to perform the skill was the cheer they would get from their friends. The excitement and care for each other completely outweighed any fear of being the only one who didn't achieve the skill. Fear could have been used as a motivator and the gymnasts may still have achieved the skill, but I guarantee fear is not a sustainable motivator and will most likely lead to mental blocks down the road. Fear closes our minds to possibility. In the above example, the group of gymnasts not only achieved their skill goals but grew in their friendships and had learnt how to encourage and support each other.

As a coach, you are a leader and mentor and have enormous power to do good in the lives of your athletes. An athlete's friends also have great, and possibly limitless, influence on their peers. You are in a position to foster young people to also use this power for good. As a coach, having a positive effect on one athlete and teaching them skills to succeed in their sport and life is an amazing achievement. If, however, you can empower an athlete to positively affect others around them, you are now able to have a positive influence that reaches much further. In a group setting this is one of the most valuable skills you can pass on to your athletes. It is so important to be intentional about how and what you teach your athletes about social interaction. I try to think about this in a couple of ways.

Being Supportive

When times are tough in life there is nothing like a bit of honest and genuine support from a friend. Teaching your athletes to be supportive of each other and repeatedly encouraging this behavior, will set them up to know the value of support and how this can be used to help others. You are teaching both a valuable lesson for life, as well as a skill that can significantly improve the performance of all your athletes in the short and long term. Sport can be tough. There are scary skills, tired bodies to push through, loses at competition or games to deal with. All tough things that can really bring people down, make them anxious and can lead to poor performance. As a coach you can offer full support and make sure they know you are proud of them. More importantly you can teach all your athletes to support each other and lean on each other as friends. If you can help create a bond that is strong enough, often the support they give each other through those hard times will exceed the support you provide as a coach. Think of it in context of your own life, perhaps when your parents or someone of authority tells you something, you are more likely to take it with a grain of salt. But when your closest friends say the same thing to you, you probably believe them almost instantly. Encouraging athletes to be supportive of each other and allow them some social time to build relationships, balanced with the many hours of hard training, can deliver powerful outcomes for the future.

Taking Responsibility

There is one sure way to ruin a friendship and that is to blame your friend for something you've done. Regardless of context or fault, friendships always struggle when people are playing the blame game and pointing the finger. It is extremely important to own your mistakes and take responsibility for them. When someone gets defensive about something, the human reaction is to start mistrusting them and questioning their integrity. This is often true regardless of the facts. The opposite is true when someone owns up to their mistakes and takes responsibility. Culturally we have a lot more respect for those people and we are more likely to trust their word in the future. It's important that we teach our athletes to learn this quality of taking ownership and responsibility for their training, their lives and for the mistakes they make. I try to teach my gymnasts that, within reason, it's better to own a mistake with your peers rather than getting caught up in the blame game. People are much more likely to respect them that way than if they are defensive and have a guarded reaction to a mistake that has been made.

I use this in business on a regular basis too. Whenever someone in my team makes a mistake, I make sure to take the responsibility for it. Not just because they're 'my team', but because it's the right thing to build team relationships. Imagine you make a mistake and your leader's boss finds out. They go to your leader to find out what's happened and you're in the room. The boss is angry and wants to know the details of whose fault it was. Let me tell you the amazing impact that comes when your leader says it was their fault instead of blaming you. The boss feels better because the leader has taken ownership, and you're filled with a huge motivation to actually fix things for them. I have never seen people react badly to this kind of behavior. The truth is everyone just wants their people to perform well, and most people given the opportunity want to rectify their mistakes. You want to strive for a culture where people genuinely learn from mistakes and are not condemned for them. If you know that you have your leaders support, a drive for excellence comes from a positive place and not a fearful one.

To teach your athletes this lesson, the easiest way of course is to tell them. Is there anything more important as a coach or teacher than to educate your athletes? So of course, teaching them about the values of being a good human being is part of the job. There's something even more important than just telling them about it, you must also model the behaviors yourself. I think owning up to your mistakes as a coach is something that needs great attention within any sport. This is certainly not a behavior I hear being modeled in most coaching settings and that has been really problematic for athlete's experiences. When modeling to your athletes that we all make mistakes, you are also showing your athletes that no one is perfect. The strive to perfection can be a lonely, destructive and unrealistic path for athletes, that leads to failure and mental struggles. No one is perfect. There are no perfect athletes out there and no perfect coaches. If people in positions of authority and mentorship expect perfection of ourselves, then we set up those looking to us for failure. By owning up to our mistakes, we show our athletes that it's ok to fail. The lesson is, it's acceptable to not be perfect and when you make a mistake you own it, learn from it and move on. Mistakes dealt with properly give your athletes the tools to grow.

I made some of my best friends when I was a gymnast and they remain my friends today. These friends have supported me and been there for me my whole life, in the good times and the bad. We are always there for each other and always will be. It's the development of this sort of relationship between the athletes that will support them in having healthy and sustainable training habits. These habits will also likely encourage them to stay in the sport long term. Allowing a little bit of social time, and encouraging genuine friendship amongst your athletes, is a truly special tool we have as coaches in creating successful athletes.

10 BELIEF

We talk about goals and aspirations, all the time, and how it's important to break them down into achievable steps. This is absolutely true, and it is an important step on the road to success. What we don't talk about as much is the doubt that creeps in. Doubt about whether you are even capable of achieving your goals. When focusing on goals and the steps to achieve them, we absolutely must instill the belief in our athletes that they are capable of achieving their goals.

In my experience the natural human state is to doubt yourself. When you are told you are amazing at something you think 'thank you but….'. When you think of your dreams, it's normal to think of them as distant and doubt whether you'll ever achieve them.

Along the way you can criticize yourself far more than your worst enemy ever would. Perhaps we don't talk about it enough, but your own inner voice can say some pretty harsh things. It manifests doubt and encourages you to aim lower to avoid failure. What we need to focus on is that we are in control of that inner voice and therefore we have the power to change it. As coaches we can educate and empower our athletes to learn how to change their inner voices. This will lead to a much higher probability of success in sport, and an incredible tool to carry them through life.

So, what do we want an athlete's inner voice to say to them? There is no doubt that the saying 'think you can or think you can't, either way you're right' is true. When your inner voice is saying 'I can do' something, then you have an amazing ability to focus, work on it and make it a reality. In fact, studies on visualization show that the same brain regions are stimulated when you imagine an action and when you actually perform that action. Our brain can strengthen neural pathways needed to achieve movement simply by visualizing it. How incredibly powerful are our brains! In order to create a successful training visual in your mind, you need to first believe that you can achieve success.

With a bit of positive reinforcement from their coach's and peers, your athletes will start to develop the skill of visualization naturally. Teaching them about their inner voice and that they are in control of it takes time and lots of repetition. For some athletes, I sometimes ask them to name the negative and positive voices in their head separately, let's say Carol for negative and Ruby for positive. Then you can choose which voice you want to give power to. Carol is that friend that is always criticizing you for no reason and tries to tear you down. Ruby is the friend that is always uplifting you and telling you how great you are. Everyone has self-doubt in their head, but they also have the power to choose who to listen to. When Carol speaks, we have the ability to tell her to go away and likewise when Ruby speaks, we can choose to listen.

The real way to encourage a positive inner voice in your athletes is to enable their hopes and dreams to be fueled instead of extinguished. In life people will always be told the reasons they can't do something. Well-meaning people, in everyone's lives, do this unintentionally. Parents say you need to be realistic about your career, coaches say you might not make that level, school guiders make their own judgements on your abilities and recommend development pathways. At most schools, the expectation of what you're capable of achieving academically is created at such a young age. Kids are graded against particular standards and put into categories that could possibly limit their potential. There is so many pressures from every aspect of our athletes' lives. It's understandable the doubt that creeps in when trying something new. It is very likely that when your athlete is trying to perform a new skill, they're going to first think of the barriers and reasons they can't do something, instead of having a positive outlook and believing they can.

Early in my competitive coaching career I was asked to start a state stream program. I started with a group of ten young gymnasts who were classed as being at a low level at that time. Prior to this I wasn't interested in coaching at the competitive level and was much more content coaching in the recreational space, playing games and just having lots of fun. I always saw the competitive side of gymnastics as intense and possibly a bit too serious for me. I was very comfortable doing what I was doing. After all I was good at it and was one of the only gymnastics coaches I knew of, who had made a career out of coaching. I doubted that I was good enough or had the ability to coach at a state level. My boss saw it differently. He saw my ability to connect with kids and inspire them and believed that it would be not only useful but important for me to take that to coaching at the competitive level. He also knew I already had the knowledge and was capable of teaching that level. So, he told me I was good enough and encouraged me to start a new squad at the club.

Backed with the belief of my boss, I had a change of heart and suddenly felt confident and excited about starting a new group. I had to do everything from planning training times, selecting gymnasts, lesson planning and so on. Once I had planned everything it was time to identify gymnasts from our club to join the group. Rather than selecting talent, skill or ability, I chose the gymnasts who I believed deserved a shot because they loved gymnastics and it showed. I truly believed that was far more important than any skill or natural ability. So that's what I did, and so I had ten gymnasts who were extremely excited to be part of this new squad.

Before my new squad started training, I went off to several top gymnastics clubs to shadow and learn from their coaches. I wanted the best chance of getting the program right. This was an extremely valuable process that taught me a lot, but there was one thing I was told that just didn't sit well with me. One of the expert coaches I observed said to me, regarding certain difficult skills, "don't bother putting those skills in your program because they will never achieve them in the state program". Maybe it was a little bit of a rebel personality coming out in me, but the first thing I did was make sure those skills were in my program.

Now that I had the gymnasts and the program, it was time to get training underway. It was a bit of a slow start as we all got to know each other and I found my rhythm, but by the third or fourth week it felt like things were really moving. In fact, we were training hard, having loads of fun and achieving countless new skills. It seemed to be going so well that demand to join the group increased. So, I put another coach on and we increased places available in the new state squad. One thing I always kept in mind was that we were on track to achieve those skills I was told not to put in the program. This was part of the longer 5+ year plan.

Fast forward twelve months and my first eight gymnasts are ready for our first ever competition. I was adamant that we didn't look at scores so we could focus on experiencing the competition and supporting each other. I am very happy that I did that because although I felt like we did ok, my gymnasts were the bottom eight. We had come dead last. This was a bit of a surprise as I had believed in my gymnasts so much and also believed that they had been working hard, so how could they have come last? I refocused on the long-term plan and made sure to concentrate on the fact that we were going to achieve great things, eventually.

About six years later, with some success and failures along the way, here I am with a group of State Level 8 gymnasts at their first competition of the season. The year before they were in level 7 and had done reasonably well, receiving a couple of medals amongst them. Although I generally focus on my own gymnasts and wait for the results to tell me where they fit in, I immediately got the sense that this time the skill level of our gymnasts was higher than the competition. I focused as normal on my own gymnasts. Supporting them and experiencing the ear-piercing encouragement they gave to each other. We had a pretty good day with some minor errors and a couple of falls. Then it was time for the results and presentations. It was very exciting to see most of our gymnasts' medal on multiple apparatus and two placed in the top three overalls. The team results came in and we were first! We were more than eight marks ahead of the second-place team, a team of gymnasts that had previously been in the national program and had since moved to the state stream. We had finally had competitive success.

At the end of the season our team was crowned Victorian State Champions. It was at this event that it was clear my gymnasts stood out for achieving those high difficulty skills in their routines. The state competition was always a second best to the national competition, but we were a group that spent the last six years believing that we could achieve more. Even with having far less training hours per week, I only ever instilled the belief in my gymnasts that they COULD achieve anything they wanted to. It was through that belief that for years they would go back to training and work hard regardless of their competition performances.

Let me take you back to the start of that journey again for a moment. Two of my gymnasts who are twin sisters are nine years old and join the squad in its early stage. At the time they were tall kids, probably better suited to netball than gymnastics. They were adamant that they were going to the Olympics as gymnasts. At the time, I just didn't have the heart to tell them otherwise so I told them they absolutely could if they worked hard enough. I was still telling them the same thing when they were sixteen and the great thing was, they still believed it. They never made the Olympics, but they both ended up transitioning to the National program and achieved great success. Other people in their life would tell them they would never make the Olympics in gymnastics, and they weren't wrong to say that. But if I as their coach hadn't told them constantly that anything was possible, they never would have gotten as far as they did. They were always told that they could achieve their dreams, they believed they were capable and were able to overcome that inner voice and the voice of others that told them they couldn't.

This is the kind of belief that I now genuinely see in all my athletes. I believe that regardless of their background, ability, body type or any other factors, that if they really want to, they can absolutely achieve anything they want to. When we train, we train as if their dreams can come true. We work on the skills that will get them there and we train as if it's going to happen because we believe that it is possible. The lessons of self-belief that we, as coaches, can teach our athletes enables them to believe in themselves. This not only positively impacts them in their sport but in every aspect of life. I'm sure that you can't achieve anything you don't believe to be possible and you absolutely can achieve anything you dream might be possible. Short term results and quick wins, changed to long term focus and building 'best version' humans, could just change the game forever. Surely that would be the best sort of competition to 'win'.

11 SUMMARY

Have you ever noticed that most sport movies go through a similar plot? There's a person or team of underdogs struggling to succeed in their sport. Along comes an inspirational coach and within one season they suddenly beat the champions, probably to find their whole life is complete at the same time. When put this way it seems unrealistic, but when watching the movie, you get sucked in to believing it can be true. It's absolutely worth believing that something like that is possible. One of my favourite movies is The Mighty Ducks. Now I know the chances of having that much turn around in less than one hockey season is pretty low. But the moment I watch Charlie (the star of the underdog team) take the final penalty shot to win the game, I am ridiculously overwhelmed with joy. My hope for you as a coach is that although you may not have revolutionary change in just one season, you will always find moments like this, however small, that overwhelm you with pride, happiness and a feeling of success.

Recently when coaching, I had a gymnast who was extremely afraid of a skill. A skill that is actually a very simple skill for her. We spent a lot of time working through this mental block she had until one day I decided to try the art of distraction. I asked her to think about her favourite food over and over again leading up to performing the skill. Block out everything else and only think of chocolate covered almonds. She tried this and it actually worked, she performed the skill for the first time in weeks. The joy that came across her face was infectious and the whole gym erupted in a cheer to celebrate with her. This was one of those moments I was ridiculously overwhelmed with joy and it's exactly this kind of experience that drives me to be the best coach I can be. Instead of expecting a level of performance, try to treat every moment as special, every small step forward as a moment to appreciate, you will not only feel happy as a coach with this mindset but it's the way to be the best mentor and person you can be.

Here is a quick summary of the key strategies from this book:

1. Know your athletes
a. Know them as people beyond their sport
2. Praise your athletes every chance you get
3. Give feedback on a ratio of 4:1
a. Four praise points to every correction
b. Corrections should focus on what they can do (not the error itself)

4.   Believe in your athletes and be their number one fan.

Coaching can be one of the most rewarding experiences you can have. So please go out there and enjoy it for what it is, you have the power to change someone's life, for the better.

Printed in the USA
CPSIA information can be obtained
at www.ICGtesting.com
LVHW020326210624
783637LV00020B/489